The Didache

The Teaching of the Twelve Apostles

A Detailed Study Guide

With Footnotes, Historical Notes on Manuscripts

Compiled by

RR

Click to View My Book Collection

My Website:

http://www.HolyLandWithRR.com

My Play Gospel Hymns Website:

http://www.LearnPianoWithRosa.com

From the Desk of Editor

I want to take this opportunity to thank you for buying my eBook.

If you had liked my eBook, please give me a feedback and drop me a review in Amazon.

I have many other similar books like this one.

Click here to visit my Collection of Books

Connect with us in these 2 Websites & Facebook:

Holy Land With RR Website

Learn to Play Piano & Gospel Hymns

Like Me in Facebook

Write to us and we look forward to hear from you,
RR Publishing Company

The Teaching of the Twelve Apostles
Commonly Called

The Didache

With Historical Notes on Manuscripts

& A Detailed Study Guide

Table of Contents

I. From the Desk of Editor

II. Table of Contents

III. Detailed Historical Manuscripts

IV. A Study Guide To Didache

V. Chapter 1

VI. Chapter 2

VII. Chapter 3

VIII. Chapter 4

IX. Chapter 5

X. Chapter 6

XI. Chapter 7

XII. Chapter 8

XIII. Chapter 9

XIV. Chapter 10

XV. Chapter 11

XVI. Chapter 12

- XVII. Chapter 13
- XVIII. Chapter 14
- XIX. Chapter 15
- XX. Chapter 16

Detailed Historical Manuscripts

The Didache(prounced "dih-dah-KAY" or sometimes "dih-dah-KEY") is also called the "Teaching of the Twelve Apostles", written around 65 - 80 A.D. The treatise is supposed to be what the twelve apostles taught to the Gentiles concerning life and death, church order, fasting, baptism, prayer, etc.

There is a debate as to its authenticity. This work is cited by Eusebius (260 – 341) and Athanasius (293-373). Origen (185 – 254) also made reference to Didache.

In the Didache, 16:2-3 is quoted in the Epistle of Barnabbas in 4:9, or vice versa. The Epistle of Barnabbas was written in 130-131 A.D. The Didache is not inspired in the Scripture, but it is a valuable early church document.

Didache was originally written in Greek and translated by Charles H. Hoole. The complete text of the Didache was discovered in the *Codex Hierosolymitanus,* though a number of other fragments exist, most notably in the Oxyrhynchus Papyri.

Manuscripts

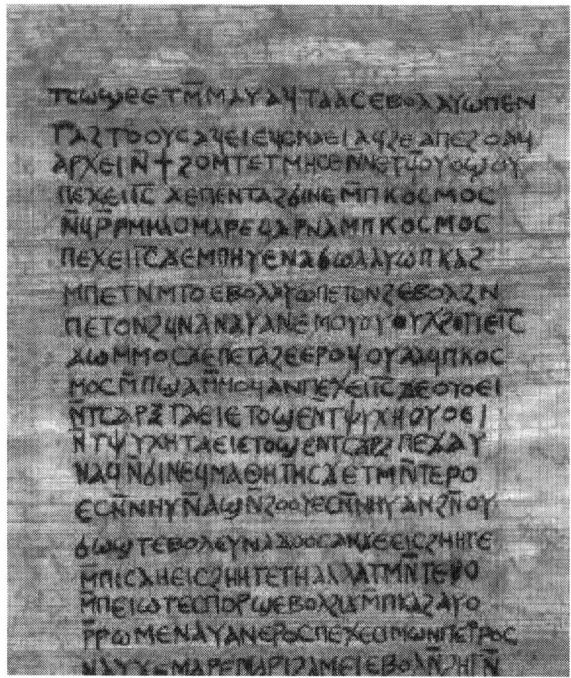

Only one Greek text of the Didache has survived. It is the Jerusalem Codex discovered by Byrennios in 1873, and published by him in Constantinople ten years later. It was written by a scribe, Leo, in 1056. A photographic facsimile was published by J. Rendel Harris in 1887.

Two papyrus fragments of the Didache in Greek (chs. 1:3, 4 and 2:7 to 3:2) were edited by A. S. Hunt in *Oxyrhynchus Papyri,* 15, London, 1922, pp. 12–15.

The Greek texts of the Epistle of Barnabas (chs. 18 to 20) and of the Apostolic Church Order (chs. 1 to 13) contain the "Two Ways" material in different forms. In the latter case there are many additions, and dependence on the "Two Ways" breaks off at the equivalent of Did. 4:8. The Greek text of the Apostolic Constitutions (ch. 7:1–32) contains almost the whole of the Didache with a number of changes and many insertions.

In Syriac there are citations from the Didache in the Didascalia, edited by R. H. Connolly, Oxford University Press, London, 1929.

In Latin there is a third century translation of the "Two Ways." A fragment was published by B. Pez in 1723. The complete text was edited from an eleventh century manuscript by J. Schlecht, *Doctrina XII Apostolorum,* Freiburg, 1900.

In Coptic there is a fifth century papyrus fragment of chs. 10:3b to 12:2a, edited by G. Horner in *The Journal of Theological Studies,* 25, 1924, pp. 225–231. (It is notable for adding after the Eucharistic prayer a thanksgiving for myron, holy oil for confirmation.)

In Arabic the "Two Ways" material is found in the fifth century *Life of Schnudi.* A German rendering is given by L. E. Iselin and A. Heusler in Texte und Untersuchungen, XIII, 1b, pp. 6–10, 1895.

In Ethiopic the following parts of the Didache have been preserved in the Ecclesiastical Canons: chs. II:3–5, 7–11, 12; 12:1–5; 13:1, 3–7; 8:1, 2a, in that order. They are edited by G. Horner, *Statutes of the Apostles*, pp. 193, 194, London, 1904.

In Georgian there is a complete translation made in the fifth century by a scribe, Jeremias of Orhai. The variant readings were published by G. Peradze in *Zeitschrift für die neutestamentliche Wissenschaft*, pp. 111–116, 1932, from a copy of an eleventh century manuscript in Constantinople.

Books and Articles

The best Greek text, making use of all the available witnesses, is by Theodorus Klauser, *Doctrina Duodecim Apostolorum: Barnabae Epistula*, "Florilegium Patristicum," I, Bonn, 1940. It has been used for this translation. Also of importance are the texts in K. Bihlmeyer, *Die apostolischen Väter*, Tübingen, 1924 (note his treatment of the Coptic evidence pp. xviii–xx), in K. Lake, *The Apostolic Fathers*, London, 1912, and in H. Hemmer, G. Oger, and A. Lamont, *Les Pères apostoliques*, Vol. I, Paris, 1907 (based on the text of F. X. Funk, *Patres apostolici*, Tübingen, 1901).

Older editions of the Didache, which contain a number of the related documents along with the text of Byrennios, are by A. Harnack, *Die Lehre der Zwölf Apostel*, Texte und Untersuchungen, II, Leipzig, 1884 (a pioneer and monumental work which includes the Greek text of the A. C. O. and the relevant parts of A. C. 7); and by Philip Schaff, *The Oldest Church Manual Called the Teaching of the Twelve Apostles*, New York, 1885 (includes the pertinent sections from Barnabas, Hermas, A. C. O., and A. C. 7).

In addition to the works of Schaff and Lake mentioned above, the following translations in English may be noted: C. Bigg, *The Doctrine of the Twelve Apostles* (revised by A. J. Maclean), London, 1922; F. X. Glimm, *The Apostolic Fathers*, in the series The Fathers of the Church, Cima Publishing Company, New York, 1947; J. A. Kleist, *The Didache, The Epistle of Barnabas*, etc., in the series Ancient

Christian Writers, Newman Press, Westminster, Maryland, 1948; and E. Goodspeed, *The Apostolic Fathers: An American Translation*, New York, 1950.

In German there are renderings by F. Zeller, *Die apostolischen Väter,* Munich, 1918, in the 2d series of the Bibliothek der Kirchenväter; by R. Knopf, *Die Lehre der Zwölf Apostel: Die zwei Clemensbriefe,* Tübingen, 1920, in Handbuch zum N. T.; and by E. Hennecke, *Neutestamentliche Apocryphen,* 2d edition, Tübingen, 1924.

In French there is the translation by Hemmer, Oger, and Lamont already mentioned.

In Italian there are renderings by M. dal Pra, *La Didache,* Venice, 1938; and by G. Bosio, *I Padri apostolici,* Part I, Turin, 1940, in the series Corona Patrum Salesiana.

All these editions have introductions and notes. The most significant are by Harnack, Schaff, Hemmer, Bigg, Kleist, and Knopf. While Klauser's introduction and notes (in Latin) are most concise, they are no less important.

Studies in the Didache are extremely numerous. Of special importance are the following books: C. Taylor, *The Teaching of the Twelve Apostles with Illustrations from the Talmud,* Cambridge, 1886; J. A. Robinson, *Barnabas, Hermas, and the Didache,* London, 1920 (a revision of chs. 1 and 3 was published posthumously with a preface by R. H. Connolly in *The Journal of Theological Studies,* 1934, pp. 113–146, 225–248); J. Muilenburg, *The Literary Relations of the Epistle of Barnabas and the Teaching of the Twelve Apostles,* Ph.D. thesis, Marburg, 1929; F. E. Vokes, *The Riddle of the Didache,* S.P.C.K., London, 1938.

For many years debate about the Didache has been carried on in *The Journal of Theological Studies.* The following articles are noteworthy: J. V. Bartlet, "The Didache Reconsidered," 1921, pp. 239–249; R. H. Connolly, "The Use of the Didache in the Didascalia," 1923, pp. 147–157; F. R. M. Hitchcock, "Did Clement of Alexandria Know the Didache?" *ibid.*, pp. 397–401; R. H. Connolly, "New Fragments of the Didache," 1924, pp. 151–153; F. C. Burkitt, "Barnabas and the Didache," 1932, pp. 25–27; R. H. Connolly, "The Didache in Relation to the Epistle of Barnabas," *ibid.*, pp. 237–253; C. T. Dix, "Didache and Diatessaron," 1933, pp. 242–250, with Connolly's reply, *ibid.*, pp. 346, 347; A. L. Williams, "The Date of the Epistle of Barnabas," *ibid.*, pp. 337–346; R. D. Middleton, "The Eucharistic Prayers of the Didache," 1935, pp. 259–267; H. G. Gibbins, "The Problem of the Liturgical Section of the Didache," *ibid.*, pp. 373–386; B. H. Streeter, "The Much-belaboured Didache," 1936, pp. 369–374; R. H. Connolly, "Barnabas and the Didache," 1937, pp. 165–167; and "Canon Streeter on the Didache," *ibid.*, pp. 364–379; J. M. Creed, "The Didache," 1938, 370–387; W. Telfer, "The Didache and the Apostolic Synod of Antioch," 1939, pp. 133–146, 258–271; J. E. L. Oulton,

"Clement of Alexandria and the Didache," 1940, pp. 177–179; W. Telfer, "The 'Plot' of the Didache," 1944, pp. 141–151.

To these studies should be added K. Kohler's article "Didache" in the *Jewish Encyclopedia*, Vol. IV, 1903, pp. 585–588; Louis Finkelstein, "The Birkat Ha-Mazon," in *Jewish Quarterly Review*, 1928, pp. 211–262; C. H. Turner, "The Early Christian Ministry and the Didache" in his *Studies in Early Church History*, Oxford, 1912, pp. 1–32; B. H. Streeter's summary of his view in *The Primitive Church* (Appendix C), New York, 1929; R. H. Connolly, "The Didache and Montanism," and "Agape and Eucharist in the Didache," both in the *Downside Review*, 1937, pp. 339–347, 477–489; the treatment by H. Lietzmann in *The Beginnings of the Christian Church*, New York, 1937, pp. 270–274; and the important study by E. Goodspeed, "The Didache, Barnabas, and the Doctrina," in the *Anglican Theological Review*, 1945, pp. 228–247, reprinted in his *Apostolic Fathers: An American Translation*, New York, 1950, pp. 285–310.

Of German and French studies we may mention A. Harnack, *Die Apostellehre und die jüdischen zwei Wege*, Leipzig, 1886, 2d edition, 1896 (an expanded reprint of his article "Apostellehre" in *Realencyclopädie für protestantische Theologie und Kirche)*; F. X. Funk, "Die Didache, Zeit und Verh ltnis zu den verwandten Schriften," and "Zur Didache, der Frage nach der Grundschrift und ihren Rezensionen," in *Kirchengeschichtliche Abhandlungen und Untersuchungen*, 2, Paderborn, 1907, pp. 108–141, 218–229; L. Wohleb, *Die lateinische Übersetzung der Didache kritisch und sprachlich untersucht*, Paderborn, 1913; M. Dibelius, "Die Mahlgebete der Didache," in *Zeitschrift für die neutestamentliche Wissenschaft*, 1938, pp. 32–41; and H. Leclercq, "Didache," in *Dictionnaire d'archéologie chrétienne et de liturgie*, Vol. IV. I, Paris, 1920, cols. 772–798. For further notices of the literature see Leclercq; also A. Harnack, *Geschichte der altchristlichen Literatur*, Leipzig, 1893, Vol. I, pp. 86–92; O. Bardenhewer, *Geschichte der altkirchlichen Literatur*, Freiburg, 1913, Vol. I, pp. 90–103; B. Altaner, *Patrologie*, 2d edition, Freiburg, 1950, pp. 39, 40; and J. Quasten, *Patrology*, Vol. I, pp. 38, 39, Utrecht, 1950.

A Study Guide To Didache

> From the Διδαχὴ τῶν Δώδεκα Ἀποστόλων (circ. A.D. 90).
>
> Κεφ. θ'. Περὶ δὲ τῆς εὐχαριστίας, οὕτως εὐχαριστήσατε· πρῶτον περὶ τοῦ ποτηρίου· Εὐχαριστοῦμέν σοι, Πάτερ ἡμῶν, ὑπὲρ τῆς ἁγίας ἀμπέλου Δαβὶδ τοῦ παιδός σου, ἧς ἐγνώρισας ἡμῖν διὰ Ἰησοῦ τοῦ παιδός σου· σοὶ ἡ δόξα εἰς τοὺς αἰῶνας. Περὶ δὲ τοῦ κλάσματος· Εὐχαριστοῦμέν σοι, Πάτερ ἡμῶν, ὑπὲρ τῆς ζωῆς καὶ γνώσεως, ἧς ἐγνώρισας ἡμῖν διὰ Ἰησοῦ τοῦ παιδός σου· σοὶ ἡ δόξα εἰς τοὺς αἰῶνας. Ὥσπερ ἦν τοῦτο κλάσμα διεσκορπισμένον ἐπάνω τῶν ὀρέων καὶ συναχθὲν ἐγένετο ἕν, οὕτω συναχθήτω σου ἡ ἐκκλησία ἀπὸ τῶν περάτων τῆς γῆς εἰς τὴν σὴν βασιλείαν· ὅτι σοῦ ἐστιν ἡ δόξα καὶ ἡ δύναμις διὰ Ἰησοῦ Χριστοῦ εἰς τοὺς αἰῶνας. Μηδεὶς δὲ φαγέτω μηδὲ πιέτω ἀπὸ τῆς εὐχαριστίας ὑμῶν, ἀλλ' οἱ βαπτισθέντες εἰς ὄνομα Κυρίου· καὶ γὰρ περὶ τούτου εἴρηκεν ὁ Κύριος· Μὴ δῶτε τὸ ἅγιον τοῖς κυσί.
>
> Κεφ. ί. Μετὰ δὲ τὸ ἐμπλησθῆναι οὕτως εὐχαριστήσατε· Εὐχαριστοῦμέν σοι, Πάτερ ἅγιε, ὑπὲρ τοῦ ἁγίου ὀνόματός σου, οὗ κατεσκήνωσας ἐν ταῖς καρδίαις ἡμῶν, καὶ ὑπὲρ τῆς γνώσεως καὶ πίστεως καὶ ἀθανασίας, ἧς ἐγνώρισας ἡμῖν διὰ Ἰησοῦ τοῦ παιδός σου· σοὶ ἡ δόξα εἰς τοὺς αἰῶνας. Σύ, δέσποτα παντοκράτορ, ἔκτισας τὰ πάντα ἕνεκεν τοῦ ὀνόματός σου, τροφήν τε καὶ ποτὸν ἔδωκας τοῖς ἀνθρώποις εἰς ἀπόλαυσιν· ἵνα σοι εὐχαριστήσωσιν, ἡμῖν δὲ ἐχαρίσω πνευματικὴν τροφὴν καὶ ποτὸν καὶ ζωὴν αἰώνιον διὰ τοῦ παιδός σου. Πρὸ πάντων εὐχαριστοῦμέν σοι ὅτι δυνατὸς εἶ· σοὶ ἡ δόξα εἰς τοὺς αἰῶνας. Μνήσθητι, Κύριε, τῆς ἐκκλησίας σου τοῦ

The *Didache* is probably the oldest surviving extant piece of Christian literature that did not make it into the canon. No document of the early church has proved so bewildering to scholars as this apparently innocent tract which was discovered by Philotheos Byrennios in 1873.

This is a handbook for new Christian converts in the 1st Century. The treatise is packed with instructions derived directly from the teachings of Jesus that were practiced in the early church.

The Didache is a first century denominational *Manual* or *Discipline*.

2 Major Themes

The Didache or Teaching (for that is what the Greek word means) falls into two major themes.

The first is a code of Christian morals, presented as a choice between the way of life and the way of death.

The second part is a manual of Church Order which, in a well-arranged manner, lays down some simple, at times even naïve, rules for the conduct of a rural congregation. It deals with such topics as baptism, fasting, the Lord's Supper, itinerant prophets, and the local ministry of bishops and deacons. It concludes with a warning paragraph on the approaching end of the world.

At one time this tract was viewed as a very ancient product—as early as A.D. 70 or 90. Recent study, however, has conclusively shown that, in the form we have it, it belongs to the second century.

A. There are Three sections to Didache:

1. Section One: Chapters 1 to 6

The first six chapters are catechetical lessons that were probably orally recited by a "membership Mentor" to a candidate for baptism/membership in the church—perhaps the mentee was required to memorize it too.

The first part of the *Didache Teaching* sets forth the duty of the Christian.

The first chapter contains "The Way of Life is the love of God and of our neighbour." The latter only is spoken of at length.

We first find the Golden Rule in the negative form. Then short extracts from the Sermon on the Mount, together with a curious passage on giving and receiving, which is cited with variations by Hermas (Mand., ii, 4-6). The Latin omits ch. i, 3-6 and ch. ii, 1, and these sections have no parallel in Barnabas; they may therefore be a later addition, and Hermas and the present text of the Didache may have used a common source, or Hermas may be the original.

The second chapter contains the Commandments against murder, adultery, theft, coveting, and false witness - in this order - and additional recommendations depending on these.

In chapter 3, we are told how one vice leads to another: anger to murder, concupiscence to adultery, and so forth.

This section shows some close likenesses to the Babylonian Talmud.

The whole chapter is passed over in Barnabas. A number of precepts are added in chapter 4 which ends: "This is the Way of Life." The Way of Death is a mere list of vices to be avoided (v).

Chapter 5 exhorts to the keeping in the Way of this Teaching: "If thou canst bear the whole yoke of the Lord, thou wilt be perfect; but if thou canst not, do what thou canst. But as for food, bear what thou canst; but straitly avoid things offered to idols; for it is a service of dead gods."

Many take this to be a recommendation to abstain from flesh, as some explain Rom. 14:2. But the "let him eat herbs" of St. Paul is a hyperbolical expression like I Cor.8:13: "I will never eat flesh, lest I should scandalize my brother", and gives no support to the notion of vegetarianism in the Early Church.

The Didache is referring to Jewish meats. The Latin version substitutes for Chapter 6 a similar close, omitting all reference to meats and to *idolothyta*, and concluding with *per d. n. j. C . . . . in sÊcula sÊculorum, amen*. This is the end of the translation.

The content of the teaching reflects the Sermon on the Mount. The citations from the Scriptures resemble those of the Apostolic Fathers. The Gospel of Matthew is most frequently used, especially chapters 4 and 6. Some of the passages fairly imply a knowledge of the Gospel of Luke.

There are some remarkable correspondences with expressions and thoughts found in the Gospel of John, while there is good reason for inferring the writer's acquaintance with all the groups of Pauline Epistles. His allusions to the other New-Testament books are less marked. There is nothing to prove that he did not know all of our canonical books. If an early date is accepted, the tone of the whole opposes the tendency-theory of the Tübingen school.

The most striking internal phenomena are, however, the correspondences of this document with early Christian writings, from A.D. 125 to the fourth century. With the so-called *Epistle to* Barnabas, chaps. xviii.-xx., the resemblances demand a critical theory which can account for them.

A few passages in the *Shepherd of Hermas* show some resemblance; but only two sentences, in Commandment Second, are verbally the same.

There is a still greater agreement with the so-called *Apostolical Church Order*, of Egyptian origin, probably as old as the third century. It is now known in the Coptic (Memphitic), and also in Arabic and Greek.

The first thirteen canons correspond quite closely, both in order and words, with Didache T*eaching* of chapters 1 to 4.

Most noteworthy, however, is the parallel with the *Apostolic Constitutions*, vii. 1–32, which contain more than half the *Teaching*, in precisely the same order, with very close in verbal resemblances.

The parts omitted are in most cases such as had lost their pertinence in the fourth century, while they seem appropriate to a much earlier period.

2. **Section Two: Chapters 7-10**

The second section gives the richest descriptions of the first century church's worship and liturgy, including baptism, fasting and communion. This section is related to the service of "first communion" the new convert received.

Chapter 7 begins with an instruction on baptism, which is to be conferred "in the Name of the Father, and of the Son and of the Holy Ghost" in living water, if possible. If not, baptism is conducted in cold or even hot water.

The baptized and, if possible, the baptizer, and other persons must fast for one or two days previously.

If the water is insufficient for immersion, it may be poured three times on the head. This is said by Bigg to show a late date; but it seems a natural concession for hot and dry countries, when baptism was not as yet celebrated exclusively at Easter and Pentecost and in churches, where a *columbethra* and a supply of water would not be wanting.

Chapter 8 talks about the Fasts. Fasts are not to be on Monday and Thursday "with the hypocrites" (i.e. the Jews), but on Wednesday and Friday. Nor must Christians pray with the hypocrites, but they shall say the Our Father three times a day.

The text of the prayer is not quite that of St. Matthew, and it is given with the doxology "for Thine is the power and the glory for ever", whereas all but a few MSS. of St. Matthew have this interpolation with "the kingdom and the power" etc.

Chapter 9 says: "Concerning the Eucharist, thus shall you give thanks: 'We give Thee thanks, our Father, for the holy Vine of David Thy Child, which Thou hast made known to us through Jesus Thy Child; to Thee be the glory for ever'. And of the broken Bread: 'We give Thee thanks, our Father, for the Life and knowledge which Thou hast made known to us through Jesus Thy Child; to Thee be glory for ever.

For as this broken Bread was dispersed over the mountains, and being collected became one, so may Thy Church be gathered together from the ends of the earth into Thy kingdom, for Thine is the glory and the power through Jesus Christ for ever.' And let none eat or drink of your Eucharist but those who have been baptized in the Name of Christ; for of this the Lord said: 'Give not the holy Thing to the dogs'."

These are clearly prayers after the Consecration and before Communion.

Chapter 10 gives a thanksgiving after Communion, slightly longer, in which mention is made of the "spiritual food and drink and eternal Life through Thy Child". After a doxology, as before, come the remarkable exclamations: "Let grace come, and this world pass away! Hosanna to the Son of David! If any is holy, let him come. If any be not, let him repent. Maranatha. Amen". We are not only reminded of the *Hosanna* and *Sancta sanctis* of the liturgies, but also of Apoc., xxii, 17, 20, and I Cor 16:22.

In these prayers we find deep reverence, and the effect of the Eucharist for eternal Life, though there is no distinct mention of the Real Presence. The words in thanksgiving for the chalice are echoed by Clement of Alexandria, "Quis div.", 29: "It is He [Christ] Who has poured out the Wine, the Blood of the Vine of David, upon our wounded souls"; and by Origen, "In i Judic.", Hom. vi: "Before we are inebriated with the Blood of the True Vine Which ascends from the root of David."

The mention of the chalice before the bread is in accordance with St. Luke, 22:17-19, in the "Western" text (which omits verse 20), and is apparently from a Jewish blessing of wine and bread, with which rite the prayers in chapter 9 have a close affinity.

3. Section 3 Chapters 11 – 17

The final six chapters outline the church organization including how to treat wandering prophets. This section gives advice respecting church officers, extraordinary and local, and the reception of Christians. The closing chapters enjoin watchfulness in view of the coming of Christ.

Chapter 11 speaks of teachers or doctors (*didaskaloi*) in general. These are to be received if they teach the above doctrine; and if they add the justice and knowledge of the Lord they are to be received as the Lord. Every Apostle is to be received as the Lord, and he may stay one day or two, but if he stay three, he is a false prophet. On leaving he shall take nothing with him but bread. If he ask for money, he is a false prophet.

Similarly with the order of prophets: to judge them when they speak in the spirit is the unpardonable sin; but they must be known by their morals. If they seek gain, they are to be rejected.

All travellers who come in the name of the Lord are to be received, but only for two or three days; and they must exercise their trade, if they have one, or at least must not be idle. Anyone who will not work is a *Christemporos* - one who makes a gain out of the name of Christ. Teachers and prophets are worthy of their food. Firstfruits are to be given to the prophets, "for they are your High Priests; but if you have not a prophet, give the firstfruits to the poor".

There is a command in which commentators have found difficult to interpret, and that is, a prophet speaking in the spirit must not be proved nor tested. "Every sin shall be forgiven, but not that." Yet there follow marks for discerning the false prophet from the true. The subsequent history of Montanism casts a clear light on the subject. The bishops attempted to test the Montanist prophetesses by applying to them the formulae of exorcism, to find whether it were possible to cast out an evil spirit who possessed them. This the Montanists naturally resisted as a frightful indignity. Such testing by exorcism is here manifestly forbidden, as involving, if applied to one really inspired by the Spirit of God, the risk of incurring the penalties denounced by our Lord, in words plainly here referred to, upon blasphemy against the Holy Ghost. That this precept of the *Didaché* was apparently not quoted in the Montanist disputes is one of many indications that our document had only a very limited circulation. Hilgenfeld's notion, that the *Didaché* is as late as Montanism, is condemned both by the whole character of the document and by its silence on the vital question in the Montanist controversy, whether true prophets lost their self-command when prophesying. To label every early document which speaks of prophesying Montanistic is to ignore the fact that prophetical gifts were recognized in the early church, and that Montanism was an unsuccessful local attempt to revive pretensions to them after they had generally ceased to be regarded as an ordinary feature of church life.

The *Didaché* gives a different way of discerning the false prophet from the true, viz. by his life and conversation. If he taught the truth but did not practise it, he was a false prophet. He might, when speaking in the spirit, command gifts to be bestowed on others; but if he asked anything for himself, or gave commands in the benefit of which he was to share, he was a false prophet. But a true prophet, settling in one place, deserves his maintenance. So also does a teacher, by which apparently is meant a preacher who does not speak in prophetic ecstasy. To the prophets are to be given the first-fruits of all produce; "for they are your high priests." If there are no prophets, the first-fruits are to go to the poor.

Chapter 14 directs Christians to come together each Lord's Day to break bread and give thanks, having confessed their sins in order that their sacrifice may be pure. Those at variance must not pollute the sacrifice by coming without having been first reconciled.

> The breaking of bread and Thanksgiving [Eucharist] is on Sunday, "after you have confessed your transgressions, that your Sacrifice may be pure", and those who are at discord must agree, for this is the clean oblation prophesied by Malachias, i, 11, 14. "Ordain therefore for yourselves bishops and deacons, worthy of the Lord . . . for they also minister to you the ministry of the prophets and teachers". Notice that it is for the sacrifice that bishops and deacons are to be ordained.

Many Fathers from Justin downwards (*Trypho*, 41, 116) have seen a prediction of the Eucharistic oblation. C. xv. begins: "Elect therefore to yourselves bishops and deacons." These are to receive the same honour as the prophets and teachers, as fulfilling a like ministration. In the preceding chapters where church officers are spoken of, mention

It is possible that the section on "bishops and deacons" may have been added later when the *Didaché* assumed its present form, the editor feeling it necessary that mention should be made of the recognized names of the officers of the church in his time.

> Chapter 16. is an exhortation to watch for our Lord's Second Coming, in order to be able to pass safely through the heavy trial that was immediately to precede it. This time of trial was to be signalized by the appearance of one who is called the "deceiver of the world" (κοσμοπλάνος), who should appear as God's Son and do signs and wonders, and into whose hands the earth should be delivered, so that under the trial many should be scandalized and be lost (cf. II. Thess. 2:3, 4; Rev. 12: 9; Matt 24:21, 24,).

> But then shall appear the signs of the truth: first the sign of outspreading (ἐκπετάσεως) in heaven (a difficult phrase which need not here be discussed); then the trumpet's voice (Matt. 14: 31; I. Cor. 15:52; I. Thess.4:16); thirdly the resurrection of the dead—not of all, but, as was said, the Lord shall come and all His saints with Him. Then shall the world see the Lord coming on the clouds of heaven.

> The last chapter, Chapter 17, exhorts Christians to watching and telling the signs of the end of the world.

B. Ask: Search for the answer yourself as to why Didache is not in the Canon

The alternate title of the *Didache* (Greek for "Teaching") is "The Teaching of the Twelve Apostles". They believe this came down from the original Apostles. Some believe it might be the result of the first Apostolic Council, about. 50AD, the one recorded in Acts 15.

Still others say it arose in one section of the church and spread everywhere due to its reasonable approach.

The Question we need to ask: Many early churches gave it apostolic authority, but why it did not make it into the Canon?

The strongest scholarship now believes the work in its earliest form may have circulated as early as the 60's AD though additions and modifications may have taken place even into the third century.

The work was never rejected by the Church, but was excluded from the canon.

After reading the whole treatise ask yourself: Why do you think it was not adopted into the Cannon when so many churches used it and even listed it is their own canon?

Chapter 1

1. Περὶ δὲ τῆς εὐχαριστίας, οὕτως εὐχαριστήσατε· 2. πρῶτον περὶ τοῦ ποτηρίου· Εὐχαριστοῦμέν σοι, πάτερ ἡμῶν, ὑπὲρ τῆς ἁγίας ἀμπέλου Δαυεὶδ τοῦ παιδός σου, ἧς ἐγνώρισας ἡμῖν διὰ Ἰησοῦ τοῦ παιδός σου· σοὶ ἡ δόξα εἰς τοὺς αἰῶνας. 3. περὶ δὲ τοῦ κλάσματος· Εὐχαριστοῦμέν σοι, πάτερ ἡμῶν, ὑπὲρ τῆς ζωῆς καὶ γνώσεως, ἧς ἐγνώρισας ἡμῖν διὰ Ἰησοῦ τοῦ παιδός σου. σοὶ ἡ δόξα εἰς τοὺς αἰῶνας. 4. ὥσπερ ἦν τοῦτο τὸ κλάσμα διεσκορπισμένον ἐπάνω τῶν ὀρέων καὶ συναχθὲν ἐγένετο ἕν, οὕτω συναχθήτω σου ἡ ἐκκλησία ἀπὸ τῶν περάτων τῆς γῆς εἰς τὴν σὴν βασιλείαν. ὅτι σοῦ ἐστιν ἡ δόξα καὶ ἡ δύναμις διὰ Ἰησοῦ Χριστοῦ εἰς τοὺς αἰῶνας. 5. μηδεὶς δὲ φαγέτω μηδὲ πιέτω ἀπὸ τῆς εὐχαριστίας ὑμῶν, ἀλλ' οἱ βαπτισθέντες εἰς ὄνομα κυρίου· καὶ γὰρ περὶ τούτου εἴρηκεν ὁ κύριος· Μὴ δῶτε τὸ ἅγιον τοῖς κυσί.

The Lord's Teaching to the Heathen by the Twelve Apostles:

1.1 There are two ways, one of life and one of death; and between the two ways there is a great difference.

1.2 Now, this is the way of life: "First, you must love God who made you, and second, your neighbor as yourself."[1] And whatever you want people to refrain from doing to you, you must not do to them.[2]

---

[1] Matt. 22:37–39; Lev. 19:18.

[2] Cf. Matt. 7:12.

1.3 What these maxims teach is this: "Bless those who curse you," and "pray for your enemies." Moreover, fast "for those who persecute you." For "what credit is it to you if you love those who love you? Is that not the way the heathen act?" But "you must love those who hate you,"[3] and then you will make no enemies.

1.4 "Abstain from carnal passions."[4] If someone strikes you "on the right cheek, turn to him the other too, and you will be perfect."[5] If someone "forces you to go one mile with him, go along with him for two"; if someone robs you "of your overcoat, give him your suit as well."[6] If someone deprives you of "your property, do not ask for it back."[7] (You could not get it back anyway!)

1.5 "Give to everybody who begs from you, and ask for no return."[8] For the Father wants his own gifts to be universally shared. Happy is the man who gives as the commandment bids him, for he is guiltless! But alas for the man who receives! If he receives because he is in need, he will be guiltless. But if he is not in need he will have to stand trial why he received and for what purpose. He will be thrown into prison and have his action investigated; and "he will not get out until he has paid back the last cent."[9]

1.6 Indeed, there is a further saying that relates to this: "Let your donation sweat in your hands until you know to whom to give it."[10]

---

[3] Matt. 5:44, 46, 47; Luke 6:27, 28, 32, 33.

[4] I Peter 2:11

[5] Matt. 5:39, 48; Luke 6:29.

[6] Matt. 5:40, 41.

[7] Luke 6:30.

[8] Ibid.

[9] Matt. 5:26. This whole section 5 should be compared with Hermas, Mand. 2:4–7, on which it is apparently dependent.
[10] Source unknown.

Chapter 2

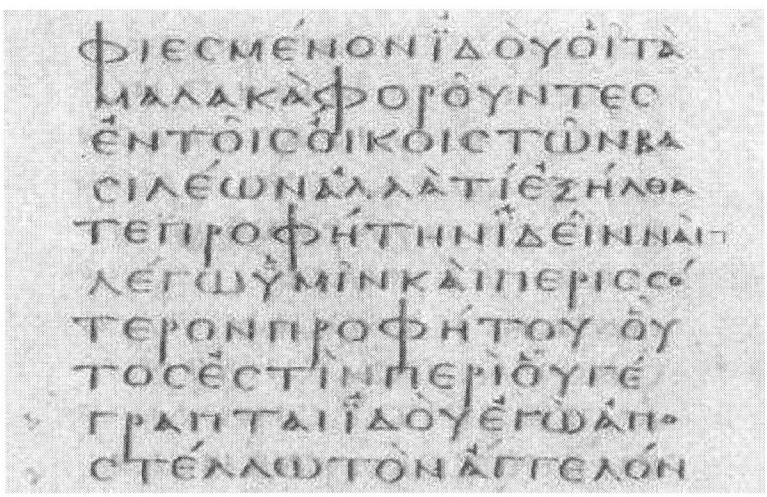

2.1 The second commandment of the Teaching:

2.2 "Do not murder; do not commit adultery"; do not corrupt boys; do not fornicate; "do not steal"; do not practice magic; do not go in for sorcery; do not murder a child by abortion or kill a new-born infant. "Do not covet your neighbor's property;

2.3 do not commit perjury; do not bear false witness";[11] do not slander; do not bear grudges.

2.4 Do not be double-minded or double-tongued, for a double tongue is "a deadly snare."[12]

2.5 Your words shall not be dishonest or hollow, but substantiated by action.

2.6 Do not be greedy or extortionate or hypocritical or malicious or arrogant. Do not plot against your neighbor.

2.7 Do not hate anybody; but reprove some, pray for others, and still others love more than your own life.

---

[11] Ex. 20:13–17; cf. Matt. 19:18; 5:33.

[12] Prov. 21:6.

Chapter 3

3.1 My child, flee from all wickedness and from everything of that sort.

3.2 Do not be irritable, for anger leads to murder. Do not be jealous or contentious or impetuous, for all this breeds murder.

3.3 My child, do not be lustful, for lust leads to fornication. Do not use foul language or leer, for all this breeds adultery.

3.4 My child, do not be a diviner, for that leads to idolatry. Do not be an enchanter or an astrologer or a magician. Moreover, have no wish to observe or heed such practices, for all this breeds idolatry.

3.5 My child, do not be a liar, for lying leads to theft. Do not be avaricious or vain, for all this breeds thievery.

3.6 My child, do not be a grumbler, for grumbling leads to blasphemy. Do not be stubborn or evil-minded, for all this breeds blasphemy.

3.7 But be humble since "the humble will inherit the earth."[13]

3.8 Be patient, merciful, harmless, quiet, and good; and always "have respect for the teaching"[14] you have been given. Do not put on airs or give yourself up to presumptuousness. Do not associate with the high and mighty; but be with the upright and humble. Accept whatever happens to you as good, in the realization that nothing occurs apart from God.

---

[13] Ps. 37:11; Matt. 5:5.

[14] Isa. 66:2.

Chapter 4

4.1 My child, day and night "you should remember him who preaches God's word to you,"[15] and honor him as you would the Lord. For where the Lord's nature is discussed, there the Lord is.

4.2 Every day you should seek the company of saints to enjoy their refreshing conversation.

4.3 You must not start a schism, but reconcile those at strife. "Your judgments must be fair."[16] You must not play favorites when reproving transgressions.

4.4 You must not be of two minds about your decision.[17]

4.5 Do not be one who holds his hand out to take, but shuts it when it comes to giving.

4.6 If your labor has brought you earnings, pay a ransom for your sins.

4.7 Do not hesitate to give and do not give with a bad grace; for you will discover who He is that pays you back a reward with a good grace.

---

[15] Heb. 13:7.

[16] Deut. 1:16, 17; Prov. 31:9.

[17] Meaning uncertain.

4.8 Do not turn your back on the needy, but share everything with your brother and call nothing your own. For if you have what is eternal in common, how much more should you have what is transient!

4.9 Do not neglect your responsibility[18] to your son or your daughter, but from their youth you shall teach them to revere God.

4.10 Do not be harsh in giving orders to your slaves and slave girls. They hope in the same God as you, and the result may be that they cease to revere the God over you both. For when he comes to call us, he will not respect our station, but will call those whom the Spirit has made ready.

4.11 You slaves, for your part, must obey your masters with reverence and fear, as if they represented God.

4.12 You must hate all hypocrisy and everything which fails to please the Lord.

4.13 You must not forsake "the Lord's commandments," but "observe" the ones you have been given, "neither adding nor subtracting anything."[19]

4.14 At the church meeting you must confess your sins, and not approach prayer with a bad conscience. That is the way of life.

---

[18] Literally, "Do not withhold your hand from . . ."

[19] Deut. 4:2; 12:32.

Chapter 5

5.1 But the way of death is this: First of all, it is wicked and thoroughly blasphemous: murders, adulteries, lusts, fornications, thefts, idolatries, magic arts, sorceries, robberies, false witness, hypocrisies, duplicity, deceit, arrogance, malice, stubbornness, greediness, filthy talk, jealousy, audacity, haughtiness, boastfulness.[20]

5.2 Those who persecute good people, who hate truth, who love lies, who are ignorant of the reward of uprightness, who do not "abide by goodness"[21] or justice, and are on the alert not for goodness but for evil: gentleness and patience are remote from them. "They love vanity,"[22] "look for profit,"[23] have no pity for the poor, do not exert themselves for the oppressed, ignore their Maker, "murder children,"[24] corrupt God's image, turn their backs on the needy, oppress the afflicted, defend the rich, unjustly condemn the poor, and are thoroughly wicked. My children, may you be saved from all this!

---

[20] Cf. Matt. 15:19; Mark 7:21, 22; Rom. 1:29–31; Gal. 5:19–21.

[21] Rom. 12:9.

[22] Ps. 4:2.

[23] Isa. 1:23.

[24] Wis. 12:6.

Chapter 6

6.1 See "that no one leads you astray"[25] from this way of the teaching, since such a one's teaching is godless.

6.2 If you can bear the Lord's full yoke, you will be perfect. But if you cannot, then do what you can.

6.3 Now about food: undertake what you can. But keep strictly away from what is offered to idols, for that implies worshiping dead gods.

---

[25] Matt. 24:4.

Chapter 7

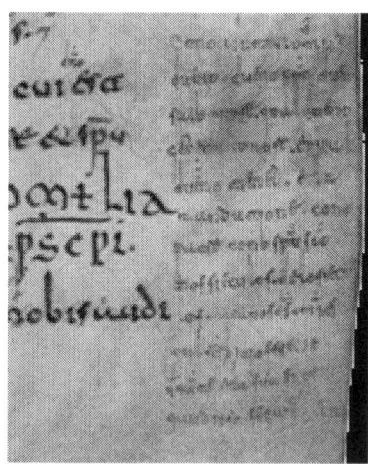

7.1 Now about baptism: this is how to baptize. Give public instruction on all these points, and then "baptize" in running water, "in the name of the Father and of the Son and of the Holy Spirit."[26]

7.2   If you do not have running water, baptize in some other.

7.3   If you cannot in cold, then in warm. If you have neither, then pour water on the head three times "in the name of the Father, Son, and Holy Spirit."[27]

7.4   Before the baptism, moreover, the one who baptizes and the one being baptized must fast, and any others who can. And you must tell the one being baptized to fast for one or two days beforehand.

---

[26] Matt. 28:19.

[27] Ibid.

Chapter 8

8.1 Your fasts must not be identical with those of the hypocrites.[28] They fast on Mondays and Thursdays; but you should fast on Wednesdays and Fridays.

8.2   You must not pray like the hypocrites,[29] but "pray as follows"[30] as the Lord bid us in his gospel:

"Our Father in heaven, hallowed be your name; your Kingdom come; your will be done on earth as it is in heaven; give us today our bread for the morrow; and forgive us our debts as we forgive our debtors. And do not lead us into temptation, but save us from the evil one, for yours is the power and the glory forever."

---

[28] I.e., the Jews. Cf. Matt. 6:16.

[29] Matt. 6:5.

[30] Cf. Matt. 6:9–13.

8.3 You should pray in this way three times a day.

Chapter 9

9.1   Now about the Eucharist:[31]   This is how to give thanks:

9.2   First in connection with the cup:[32]

"We thank you, our Father, for the holy vine[33] of David, your child, which you have revealed through Jesus, your child. To you be glory forever."

---

[31] I.e., "the Thanksgiving." The term, however, had become a technical one in Christianity for the special giving of thanks at the Lord's Supper. One might render the verbal form ("give thanks"), which immediately follows, as "say grace," for it was out of the Jewish forms for grace before and after meals (accompanied in the one instance by the breaking of bread and in the other by sharing a common cup of wine) that the Christian thanksgivings of the Lord's Supper developed.

[32] It is a curious feature of the Didache that the cup has been displaced from the end of the meal to the very beginning. Equally curious is the absence of any direct reference to the body and blood of Christ.

[33] This may be a metaphorical reference to the divine life and knowledge revealed through Jesus (cf. ch. 9:3). It may also refer to the Messianic promise (cf. Isa. 11:1), or to the Messianic community (cf. Ps. 80:8), i.e., the Church.

9.3 Then in connection with the piece[34]. [broken off the loaf]:

"We thank you, our Father, for the life and knowledge which you have revealed through Jesus, your child. To you be glory forever.

9.4 "As this piece [of bread] was scattered over the hills[35] and then was brought together and made one, so let your Church be brought together from the ends of the earth into your Kingdom. For yours is the glory and the power through Jesus Christ forever."

9.5 You must not let anyone eat or drink of your Eucharist except those baptized in the Lord's name. For in reference to this the Lord said, "Do not give what is sacred to dogs."[36]

---

[34] An odd phrase, but one that refers to the Jewish custom (taken over in the Christian Lord's Supper) of grace before meals. The head of the house would distribute to each of the guests a piece of bread broken off a loaf, after uttering the appropriate thanksgiving to God

[35] The reference is likely to the sowing of wheat on the hillsides of Judea.

[36] Matt. 7:6.

Chapter 10

10.1 After you have finished your meal, say grace[37] in this way:

10.2 "We thank you, holy Father, for your sacred name which you have lodged[38] in our hearts, and for the knowledge and faith and immortality which you have revealed through Jesus, your child. To you be glory forever.

10.3 "Almighty Master, 'you have created everything'[39] for the sake of your name, and have given men food and drink to enjoy that they may thank you. But to us you have given spiritual food and drink and eternal life through Jesus, your child.

10.4 "Above all, we thank you that you are mighty. To you be glory forever.

10.5 "Remember, Lord, your Church, to save it from all evil and to make it perfect by your love. Make it holy, 'and gather' it 'together from the four winds'[40] into your Kingdom which you have made ready for it. For yours is the power and the glory forever."

10.6 "Let Grace[41] come and let this world pass away."

---

[37] Or "give thanks." See note 47.

[38] For the phrase cf. Neh. 1:9.

[39] Wis. 1:14; Sir. 18:1; Rev. 4:11.

[40] Matt. 24:31.

[41] A title for Christ.

"Hosanna to the God of David!"[42]

"If anyone is holy, let him come. If not, let him repent."[43]

"Our Lord, come!"[44]

"Amen."[45]

10.7 In the case of prophets, however, you should let them give thanks in their own way.[46]

---

[42] Cf. Matt. 21:9, 15.

[43] Or perhaps "be converted."

[44] Cf. I Cor. 16:22.

[45] These terse exclamations may be vesicles and responses. More likely they derive from the Jewish custom of reading verses concerning Israel's future redemption and glory, after the final benediction.

[46] I.e., they are not bound by the texts given.

Chapter 11

11.1 Now, you should welcome anyone who comes your way and teaches you all we have been saying.

11.2 But if the teacher proves himself a renegade and by teaching otherwise contradicts all this, pay no attention to him. But if his teaching furthers the Lord's righteousness and knowledge, welcome him as the Lord.

11.3 Now about the apostles and prophets: Act in line with the gospel precept.[47]

---

[47] Matt. 10:40, 41.

11.4 Welcome every apostle on arriving, as if he were the Lord.

11.5 But he must not stay beyond one day. In case of necessity, however, the next day too. If he stays three days, he is a false prophet.

11.6 On departing, an apostle must not accept anything save sufficient food to carry him till his next lodging. If he asks for money, he is a false prophet.

11.7 While a prophet is making ecstatic utterances,[48] you must not test or examine him. For "every sin will be forgiven," but this sin "will not be forgiven."[49]

11.8 However, not everybody making ecstatic utterances is a prophet, but only if he behaves like the Lord. It is by their conduct that the false prophet and the [true] prophet can be distinguished.

11.9 For instance, if a prophet marks out a table in the Spirit,[50] he must not eat from it. If he does, he is a false prophet.

11.10 Again, every prophet who teaches the truth but fails to practice what he preaches is a false prophet.

---

[48] Literally, "speaking in a spirit," i.e., speaking while possessed by a divine or demonic spirit. This whole passage (ch. 11:7–12) is a sort of parallel to Matt. 12:31 ff. There is an interpretation of the sin against the Holy Ghost, followed by a comment on good and evil conduct (cf. Matt. 12:33–37), and concluded by the prophets' signs which are suggested by the sign of the Son of Man (Matt. 22:38 ff.).

[49] Matt. 12:31.

[50] The sense is not clear, but suggests a dramatic portrayal of the Messianic banquet. It was characteristic of the Biblical prophets to drive home their teaching by dramatic and symbolic actions (cf. Jer., ch. 19; Acts 21:11; etc.).

11.11 But every attested and genuine prophet who acts with a view to symbolizing the mystery of the Church,[51] and does not teach you to do all he does, must not be judged by you. His judgment rests with God. For the ancient prophets too acted in this way.

11.12 But if someone says in the Spirit, "Give me money, or something else," you must not heed him. However, if he tells you to give for others in need, no one must condemn him.

---

[51] Literally, "acts with a view to a worldly mystery of the Church." The meaning is not certain, but some dramatic action, symbolizing the mystical marriage of the Church to Christ, is probably intended. The reference may, indeed, be to the prophet's being accompanied by a spiritual sister (cf. I Cor 7:36 ff.).

Chapter 12

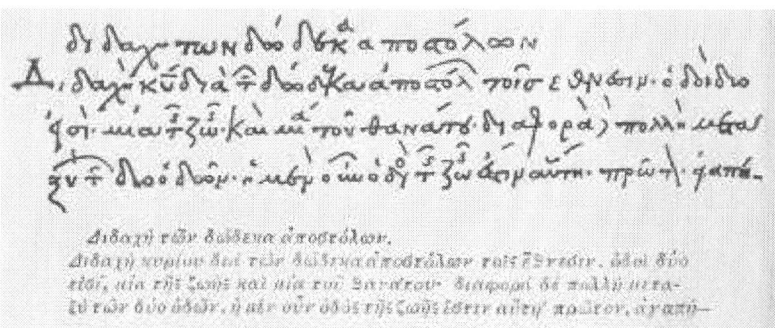

12.1 Everyone "who comes" to you "in the name of the Lord"[52] must be welcomed. Afterward, when you have tested him, you will find out about him, for you have insight into right and wrong.

12.2 If it is a traveler who arrives, help him all you can. But he must not stay with you more than two days, or, if necessary, three.

12.3 If he wants to settle with you and is an artisan, he must work for his living.

12.4 If, however, he has no trade, use your judgment in taking steps for him to live with you as a Christian without being idle.

12.5 If he refuses to do this, he is trading on Christ. You must be on your guard against such people.

---

[52] Matt. 21:9; Ps. 118:26; cf. John 5:43.

Chapter 13

Ἀργυρίου δὲ καὶ ἱματισ-
μοῦ καὶ παντὸς κτήματος
λαβὼν τὴν ἀπαρχήν ὡς ἄν
σοι δόξῃ, δὸς κατὰ τὴν
ἐντολήν. Κατὰ κυριακὴν
δὲ κυρίου συναχθέντες
κλάσατε ἄρτον καὶ
εὐχαριστήσατε ....

(Didache 13:7-14:1)

13.1   Every genuine prophet who wants to settle with you "has a right to his support."

13.2   Similarly, a genuine teacher himself, just like a "workman, has a right to his support."[53]

13.3   Hence take all the first fruits of vintage and harvest, and of cattle and sheep, and give these first fruits to the prophets. For they are your high priests.

13.4   If, however, you have no prophet, give them to the poor.

13.5   If you make bread, take the first fruits and give in accordance with the precept.[54]

13.6   Similarly, when you open a jar of wine or oil, take the first fruits and give them to the prophets.

---

[53] Matt. 10:10. The provision for the prophet or teacher to settle and to be supported by the congregation implies the birth of the monarchical episcopate. Note the connection of this with the high priesthood (cf. Hippolytus, Apost. Trad. 3:4) and tithing. No provision is made for the support of the local clergy in ch. 15.

[54] Deut. 18:3–5.

13.7 Indeed, of money, clothes, and of all your possessions, take such first fruits as you think right, and give in accordance with the precept.

Chapter 14

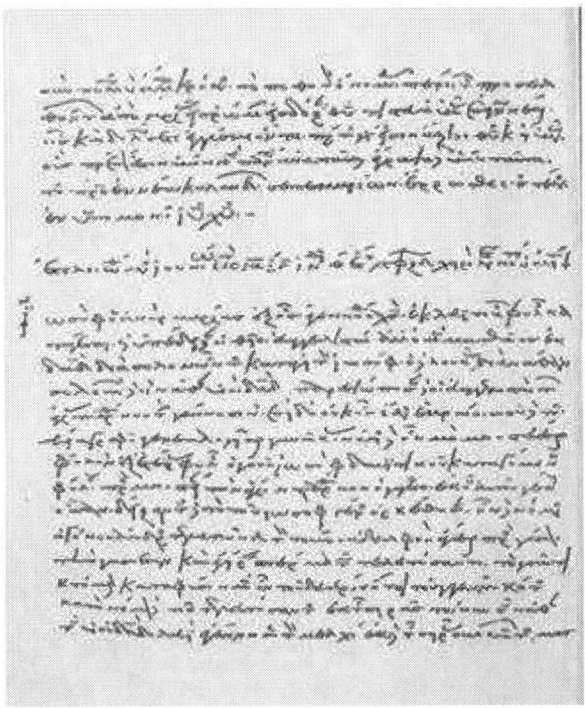

14.1 On every Lord's Day—his special day[55] — come together and break bread and give thanks, first confessing your sins so that your sacrifice may be pure.

14.2 Anyone at variance with his neighbor must not join you, until they are reconciled, lest your sacrifice be defiled.

14.3 For it was of this sacrifice that the Lord said, "Always and everywhere offer me a pure sacrifice; for I am a great King, says the Lord, and my name is marveled at by the nations."[56]

---

[55] Literally, "On every Lord's Day of the Lord."

[56] Mal. 1:11, 14.

Chapter 15

15.1 You must, then, elect for yourselves bishops and deacons who are a credit to the Lord, men who are gentle, generous, faithful, and well tried. For their ministry to you is identical with that of the prophets and teachers.

15.2 You must not, therefore, despise them, for along with the prophets and teachers they enjoy a place of honor among you.

15.3 Furthermore, do not reprove each other angrily, but quietly, as you find it in the gospel. Moreover, if anyone has wronged his neighbor, nobody must speak to him, and he must not hear a word from you, until he repents.

15.4 Say your prayers, give your charity, and do everything just as you find it in the gospel of our Lord.

Chapter 16

16.1 "Watch" over your life: do not let "your lamps" go out, and do not keep "your loins ungirded"; but "be ready," for "you do not know the hour when our Lord is coming."[57]

16.2 Meet together frequently in your search for what is good for your souls, since "a lifetime of faith will be of no advantage"[58] to you unless you prove perfect at the very last.

16.3 For in the final days multitudes of false prophets and seducers will appear.

16.4 Sheep will turn into wolves, and love into hatred. For with the increase of iniquity men will hate, persecute, and betray each other. And then the world deceiver will appear in the guise of God's Son. He will work "signs and wonders"[59] and the earth will fall into his hands and he will commit outrages such as have never occurred before.

---

[57] Matt. 24:42, 44; Luke 12:35.

[58] Barn. 4:9.

[59] Matt. 24:24.

16.5 Then mankind will come to the fiery trial "and many will fall away"[60] and perish, "but those who persevere" in their faith "will be saved"[61] by the Curse himself.[62]

16.6 Then "there will appear the signs"[63] of the Truth: first the sign of stretched-out [hands] in heaven,[64] then the sign of "a trumpet's blast,"[65] and thirdly the resurrection of the dead, though not of all the dead,

16.7 but as it has been said: "The Lord will come and all his saints with him. Then the world will see the Lord coming on the clouds of the sky."[66]

---

[60] Matt. 24:10.

[61] Matt. 10:22; 24:13.

[62] An obscure reference, but possibly meaning the Christ who suffered the death of one accursed (Gal. 3:13; Barn. 7:9). Cf. two other titles for the Christ: Grace (ch. 10:6) and Truth (v. 6).

[63] Matt. 24:30.

[64] Another obscure reference, possibly to the belief that the Christ would appear on a glorified cross. Cf Barn. 12:2–4.

[65] Matt. 24:31.

[66] Zech. 14:5; I Thess. 3:13; Matt. 24:30.

Printed in France by Amazon
Brétigny-sur-Orge, FR

42648011R00027